D0039962

A Ceremony of Marriage

Kenneth Copeland

KCP Publications
Fort Worth, Texas

A Message from Kenneth Copeland

The marriage union is the closest relationship that can exist between two human beings. When a man and woman decide to join together in marriage, they should do so with full realization of their responsibilities. Marriage is serious business.

When two born-again believers know it is God's will for them to marry, they come together before God, before a minister, and before witnesses to join their hearts and lives for eternity. They make a public profession of their mutual love and devotion, pronouncing vows and pledging their lives to each other.

As they pronounce the marriage vows in faith, the power of God goes into operation and a miracle takes place. They are united by God and become as one in His sight. Their union is threefold: They are joined together *spiritually* by God, *legally* by the contract they enter into, and *physically* when the marriage is consummated.

A husband and wife are joined together as Jesus is joined to the Church. It is a miraculous union!

This booklet contains the wedding ceremony I use as a minister of God. It is based totally and completely on the Word of God.

As you use this ceremony, I add my faith to yours in believing God for a life of love and harmony, in Jesus' name.

Kenneth Copeland

Giving of the Bride

TO FATHER: Who gives this bride in marriage?

RESPONSE: I do.

TO GROOM: Take your bride and step forward please.

TO CONGREGATION: I ask that the congregation remain standing as we go before the Lord in prayer.

"Our most gracious heavenly Father, we thank You for all the privileges of being in the Body of Christ.
"We have come together to watch the miracle of Your love and the power of Your Spirit work in the lives of these two people.
"We give You the praise, the honor, and the glory for the power of the Holy Spirit in our lives to bring us into a place of union with the Father, union with the Son, union with the Holy Spirit, and union with one another. We thank You for it, in Jesus' mighty name. Amen."

TO CONGREGATION: You may be seated.

Charge to the Bride and Groom

As I read Scripture from the fifth chapter of the Book of Ephesians, I want you both to pay very close attention to the words stated here. They are the words, from God's Word, that the Holy Spirit will honor as we stand on them in faith.

The world has the idea that marriage is simply a legal contract. It *is* a legal contract (we don't make light of that); but at the same time, it is a spiritual contract. When the words of faith are spoken according to the Word of God between two born-again believers, the power of God goes into operation. There is an actual miracle that takes place when the faith of these two people is released in God's power. God honors their faith and brings them into union together.

With these thoughts in mind, listen very carefully to these words:

> *Wives, submit yourselves unto your own husbands, as unto the Lord.*
> *For the husband is the head of the wife, even as Christ is the head of the church: and he is the saviour of the body.*
> *Therefore as the church is subject unto Christ, so let the wives be to their own husbands in every thing.*

Husbands, love your wives, even as Christ also loved the church, and gave himself for it; that he might sanctify and cleanse it with the washing of water by the word, that he might present it to himself a glorious church, not having spot, or wrinkle, or any such thing; but that it should be holy and without blemish.

So ought men to love their wives as their own bodies. He that loveth his wife loveth himself. For no man ever yet hated his own flesh; but nourisheth and cherisheth it, even as the Lord the church:

For we are members of his body, of his flesh, and of his bones.

For this cause shall a man leave his father and mother, and shall be joined unto his wife, and they two shall be one flesh. This is a great mystery: but I speak concerning Christ and the church.

TO GROOM: _____, have you accepted Jesus Christ as Lord and personal Savior?

RESPONSE: I have.

Have you received the Holy Spirit to dwell in you?

RESPONSE: I have.

TO BRIDE: _____, have you accepted Jesus Christ as Lord and personal Savior?

RESPONSE: I have.

Have you received the Holy Spirit to dwell in you?

RESPONSE: I have.

TO BRIDE AND GROOM: Now upon public profession of your faith, you have made known to all men that Jesus Christ of Nazareth is your Lord and your Savior.

I make this announcement before this congregation and these witnesses: When two people join themselves to the Lord Jesus Christ by faith, according to God's own words and God's own statement, they stand cleansed — as clean before God as Adam and Eve were in the Garden of Eden before they sinned. This is not just a forgiveness of sin. The Bible says any man who is in Christ is a new creation; old things have passed away and all things have become new.

A miracle took place when you made Jesus the Lord of your life. The Holy Spirit used the very power of God — His creative power — to cause your spirit to be reborn. It is the same power that God used when He raised Jesus from the dead, and He joined you to Jesus by that power.

When two born-again believers come before God to be joined together as husband and wife, the Apostle Paul calls it "a mystery" and says, "... but I speak concerning Christ and the church." When you made Jesus the Lord of your lives, you were joined to Him. First Corinthians 6:17 says you are one spirit with Him. Here in Ephesians, it says that you have become one flesh with the Lord. You are His. He is yours. You are one together with Him.

I want you to understand that if you rightly discern the Body of Christ, then you rightly discern the miracle that takes place in marriage. Your spirits will be joined together and you will become one. You will not be one just in the eyes of the law. There is something much more powerful that happens. The very creative power of God will join you together. The same power that joined you with Jesus when you made Him your Lord will join you together.

Don't ever tamper with that union. The love of God doesn't say, "I love you, but do you really love me?" The love of God says very simply, "I love you." That's all it ever says. Don't ever tamper with that miracle. Don't ever let the sun go down on your wrath. Something holy, something beyond reproach, will take place by the Spirit of God inside your bosom; and it is a precious thing.

TO WITNESSES: I want to speak this to the witnesses here:

Jesus said in the 18th chapter of Matthew's Gospel, "Again I say unto you, That if two of you shall agree on earth as touching any thing that they shall ask, it shall be done for them of my Father which is in heaven."

You are not here just because of tradition. You are here for a serious purpose — to bear witness forever of the miraculous union that will take place, and to add your agreement before God to that which takes place.

Don't ever, ever, ever tamper with that agreement. From this day forward, regardless of what comes, you are in agreement with this union. Don't ever attempt in any way to cause it to be anything other than a happy union.

TO CONGREGATION:

In the eyes of Almighty God, these two people are washed in the blood of the Lamb — Jesus Christ of Nazareth. They have prayed and, before the Lord God Himself, they believe with all their hearts that it is the perfect will of God for them to be joined together in the spirit. They have made their decision, so from now until the end of this age, I charge you to do everything in your power to see that this union remains solid and strong and happy and prosperous.

Woe be to any person who would tamper with it and cause it to be anything other than prosperous in the eyes of God. This is a miraculous thing, and it is of God.

Profession of Vows

TO GROOM: _____, do you take _____ as your wife, as your own flesh, to love her even as Christ loves the Church, to protect her and care for her the rest of your lives?
RESPONSE: I do.
Then turn to her and make this profession of your faith:

I, _____, according to the Word of God, leave my father and my mother and I join myself to you, to be a husband to you. From this moment forward, we shall be one.

TO BRIDE: _____, do you take _____ as your husband, submitting yourself to him as unto the Lord, showing reverence to him as the head of this union for the rest of your lives?
RESPONSE: I do.

Then turn to him and make this profession of your faith:

I, _____, according to the Word of God, submit myself to you, to be a wife to you. From this moment forward, we shall be one.

Presentation of Rings

TO GROOM: May I have the Bride's ring, please.

A ring is a very precious thing — a token of your faith and your love. This ring is made out of precious metal. It is a never-ending circle that indicates the continuing love of God — a love that never fails, never presents itself haughty nor puffed up. The love of God and the faith of God is what causes His power to move in your lives.

I want you to wear these rings as a continual reminder of your faith, a continual reminder of the confession of faith you have made to each other and to God.

The Word of God says, "Above all, take the shield of faith, wherewith ye shall be able to quench all the fiery darts of the wicked one." If anyone could break up this union, it would be Satan, so give him no place. Give him no place! This is forever.

TO GROOM: Take this ring, place it on her finger, and say this to her:

> With this ring, I thee wed. It is a token of my love for you and a token of my faith that I release now, in Jesus' name.

TO BRIDE: May I have the Groom's ring, please.

TO GROOM: A ring can mean two different things. It can be a never-ending sign of love, or it can be a shackle. I am going to charge you with a memory you should remember always: This woman stands by your side, not under your feet. You have the responsibility of being the head of this union. You have spiritual responsibility. I want you to wear this ring in remembrance that she is your helpmate. It must never be a shackle of dominance, but always a reminder of faith and love.

TO BRIDE: I want you to place this ring on his finger with these things in mind. There is no place in the Word of God that gives people the right to dominate one another. Your vows have stated that you submit to one another in the responsibilities of this life, expecting God and His power to always make the difference. So place this ring on his finger and, as you do, say this to him:

> With this ring, I thee wed. I give it as a token of my faith. I believe with all my heart that this is forever. It is my love and my faith, in the name of Jesus.

Pronouncement

TO BRIDE AND GROOM: Join right hands please.

As a representative of Jesus Christ, before Almighty God and in the name of the Father, of His Son Jesus, and by the power of the Holy Spirit of God, I now pronounce you one together. You are now husband and wife.

Communion

TO BRIDE AND GROOM: Please kneel to receive communion.

Both of you as believers have received the communion table in the past. You know what it means, but I want to remind you that we live under a covenant with God. This covenant was ratified by the shed blood of Jesus at Calvary.

Now we see something new that has never existed before. When each of you were born again, you became a new creature in Christ. The two of you together have become a new creature in Christ because you are now one. When you agree on things, they will come to pass. You have an awesome power at your disposal. You are going to notice a new realm of your life beginning because of a spiritual law that says one can put a thousand to flight, two can put ten thousand to flight. From this time forward, your everyday life will be 10,000 times more powerful spiritually than ever before.

It is important that in these first moments together you honor the Lord, honor His table.

Jesus said, "This is my body, broken for you. Eat of it."

GIVE BREAD TO COUPLE.

His precious body bore your sicknesses and carried your diseases. The two of you together in the name of Jesus Christ have the God-given faith and the God-given power to ward off sickness, disease, the storms of life, and everything that hell would offer any marriage. Through this broken body, you have received into your hands the awesome power of Almighty God.

Jesus also said, "This is My blood that ratifies the covenant. Drink of My blood and as often as you drink it, do it in remembrance of Me."

As you drink tonight, I want you to remember what He has done for you. I want you to remember the covenant that He has made available to you — the power that He has made yours.

GIVE CUP TO COUPLE.

TO BRIDE AND GROOM: You may rise.

Blessing of the Union

Galatians, chapter 3, says that Christ has redeemed us from the curse of the law, being made a curse for us, so that the blessing of Abraham might come on the Gentiles through Jesus Christ, that we might be heirs of the promise of the Spirit.

First Peter, chapter 3, says a man and his wife are heirs together of the grace of life.

I am going to read to you your blessing, your inheritance, so listen carefully.

According to Deuteronomy, chapter 28, all these blessings will come on you and overtake you, if you will hearken unto the voice of the Lord your God:

Blessed shalt thou be in the city, and blessed shalt thou be in the field.

Blessed shall be the fruit of thy body, and the fruit of thy ground, and the fruit of thy cattle, the increase of thy kine, and the flocks of thy sheep.

Blessed shall be thy basket and thy store.

Blessed shalt thou be when thou comest in, and blessed shalt thou be when thou goest out.

The Lord shall cause thine enemies that rise up against thee to be smitten before thy face: they shall come out against thee one way, and flee before thee seven ways.

The Lord shall command the blessing upon thee in thy storehouses, and in all that thou settest thine hand unto; and he shall bless thee in the land which the Lord thy God giveth thee.

The Lord shall establish thee an holy people unto himself, as he hath sworn unto thee, if thou shalt keep the commandments of the Lord thy God, and walk in his ways.

And all people of the earth shall see that thou art called by the name of the Lord; and they shall be afraid of thee.

And the Lord shall make thee plenteous in goods, in the fruit of thy body, and in the fruit of thy cattle, and in the fruit of thy ground, in the land which the Lord sware unto thy fathers to give thee.

The Lord shall open unto thee his good treasure, the heaven to give the rain unto thy land in his season, and to bless all the work of thine hand: and thou shalt lend unto many nations, and thou shalt not borrow.

And the Lord shall make thee the head, and not the tail; and thou shalt be above only, and thou shalt not be beneath; if that thou hearken unto the commandments of the Lord thy God, which I command thee this day, to observe and to do them.

Presentation to Congregation

TO BRIDE AND GROOM: Please turn and face this congregation.

TO CONGREGATION: Ladies and gentlemen, I present to you Mr. and Mrs.

_____.

A Ceremony of Marriage

ISBN 0-938458-15-9   30-0012

©1979 Kenneth Copeland Ministries, Inc.

All Rights Reserved. Reproduction in Whole or Part Without Written Permission is Prohibited. Printed in United States of America.

Unless otherwise indicated, all Scripture quotations are from the KING JAMES VERSION.

Published by KCP Publications
Fort Worth, Texas 76192